tweet inspiration

Faith in 140 Characters
(or Less)

MARK HART

SERVANT
BOOKS

PUBLISHED BY FRANCISCAN MEDIA
Cincinnati, Ohio

"In concise phrases, often no longer than a verse from the
Bible, profound thoughts can be communicated, as long
as those taking part in the conversation do not neglect to
cultivate their own inner lives."
—Pope Benedict XVI

Cover and book design by Mark Sullivan
Cover image © Veer | Anna Penigina

ISBN 978-1-61636-536-3

Published by Servant Books,
an imprint of Franciscan Media
28 W. Liberty St.
Cincinnati, Ohio 45202
www.FranciscanMedia.org
www.ServantBooks.org

Printed in the United States of America.
Printed on acid-free paper.
13 14 15 16 17 5 4 3 2 1

To the memory of Angela Faddis, whose constant fidelity and courage during her battle with cancer taught me what it means to trust God and to love like Christ *every day*. Her redemptive suffering blessed countless souls, my own very much included.

To her husband, Chris, I thank you for your witness through it all, brother. What a beautiful image you gave us of the sacrament—a living example of what makes matrimony so holy.

And, finally, to her children Gianna and Augustine (Gus), I hope you'll ask your mother to pray with you daily, and that you'll believe all that you hear of her...for she truly was a beautiful soul, and her reflection lives on in you both.

introduction

In 1951, a beloved and charismatic bishop took to the television airwaves in the United States with a singular purpose—to share the love of God through the teachings of Christ and His Church.

Venerable Fulton Sheen has become more than a Catholic icon or a personal hero. Sheen was a masterful communicator. He didn't just know the faith, he knew how to articulate it—in an unforgettable way, with passion and depth and undoubtedly with great humor. The bishop's humor was not funny for humor's sake; witty remarks were not merely a moment for a listener to catch his or her intellectual breath. No, humor was a great tool used to tear down walls and build up souls. For Sheen, humor was a tactical weapon used to engage souls chained in sin and minds trapped in darkness.

In the work of evangelization, humor is an indispensible tool. Theological debate might enrapture the mind, but humor strikes the chord of the heart with a note that carries. While some academics might dismiss pithy remarks as juvenile or satiric wit as immature, the greatest Christians—many of them saints—have reminded us that humor is, in a way, the highest form of philosophy. For if philosophy is a commentary on the collective thoughts and experience of man, humor is the commentary on that commentary. As Walt Disney put it, "Humor is our 'sixth sense.'"

Sheen's effectiveness, however, didn't stem merely from Irish wit or a working man's approachability. Sheen knew how to connect with people. Other theologians might have known the words, but it was clear that Sheen also knew the Author (see Acts 3:15). Other celebrities knew how to connect with an audience, but Sheen was a catechetical surgeon, using the Scriptures like a scalpel that cut to the heart with a pinpoint precision even more exact and piercing than a sword (see Hebrews 4:12).

At this point you might be asking yourself, "Why all this talk about Fulton Sheen? This isn't a biography."

Well, allow me to submit that you're both correct and incorrect.

True, this is not a biography about Fulton Sheen, though the ideas contained within and my personal approach toward modern evangelization—and, indeed, toward life itself—has been (upon reflection) subconsciously shaped by Venerable Fulton Sheen's works. The thoughts, comments, and quips I offer here, however, *are* a bit of a biography, I suppose…a reflection of my perspective on living as a Catholic in the modern age and a summation of my own failings, misgivings, and (often failed) attempts at living a virtuous life in this highly egocentric culture of death.

I don't share tweets about the Catholic life because I have it figured out—I share them because I don't. To be clear, I don't "tweet" because I have nothing better to do; I tweet because I have no one better to share them with.

I was initially opposed to Twitter upon its inception. "Oh, great," I thought to myself, "yet *another* social media outlet for people to disengage from reality." I had witnessed, firsthand, how many souls—young and old alike—had been sucked into the mindless and endless black hole of technology. You've seen it, too: families sitting together in a restaurant, completely disengaged from one another, not talking or making eye contact, all the while glued to their respective screens. It is a sad commentary on the state of the modern family and upon our screen-based culture in general.

Still, the Holy Spirit was prompting me during prayer to enter the "twitterverse." "How can we use these new technologies to reach souls?" I wondered. "How can we offer light into darkness in 140 characters or less (the maximum character allowance for a 'tweet')? How can we fulfill Christ's charge to carry the Gospel to the ends of the earth (Matthew 28:19) and to proclaim God's unyielding truth from the "housetops" (Matthew 10:27)?"

If St. Paul were on earth today, you'd better believe he'd have a Twitter account. He'd be on Facebook and on Instagram. He would use anything and everything at his disposal to point others toward the love and the mercy of Jesus Christ. St. Paul, like Fulton Sheen, was a master at engaging people where they were and walking them into constantly deepening encounters with Christ. Pope Benedict XVI has affirmed the need for Christians to engage in the use of social media, as well:

> When people exchange information, they are already sharing themselves, their view of the world, their hopes, their ideals. It follows that there exists a Christian way of being present in the digital world: this takes the form of a communication which is honest and open, responsible and respectful of others. To proclaim the Gospel through the new media means not only to insert expressly religious

content into different media platforms, but also to witness consistently, in one's own digital profile and in the way one communicates choices, preferences and judgments that are fully consistent with the Gospel, even when it is not spoken of specifically. Furthermore, it is also true in the digital world that a message cannot be proclaimed without a consistent witness on the part of the one who proclaims it. In these new circumstances and with these new forms of expression, Christian are once again called to offer a response to anyone who asks for a reason for the hope that is within them (cf. 1 Peter 3:15).

—Pope Benedict XVI, World Communications Day 2011

So this book of "tweets" is a collection of ideas, perspective put to paper—the catalyst some souls (myself included) might need to regain our joy or our hope or our sanity on those days when it's hard to see God's hand at work.

The thoughts contained within are for the most part my own. Some are re-articulations or re-framings of popular concepts or age-old truths that I've come across over the years or had spill out of my pen in early mornings or late nights of journaling and prayer. I pray that something within this book will spark a prayerful moment, encourage a more positive outlook, or invite God's joy into the stressful Monday, the mundane Thursday, or the hectic Saturday. As Sheen reminded us, "Joy is not the same as levity. Levity is an act; joy, a habit."

You'll notice that certain tweets have a slightly longer commentary. While Twitter is wonderful in its character limit—forcing an economy of words that sharpens the message and challenges the writer—it's not always enough in matters of faith and morals. I could easily have expounded on every single entry. As it is, I expounded only on the ideas the Holy Spirit directed me toward.

In the end, I pray that the reflections here mirror what Sacred Scripture itself does…that these words will comfort the afflicted and afflict the comfortable. Let me be clear, when I write these things, I'm speaking to myself, first. I am just a sinner seeking my Savior. I'm trying to find God in my "every day," and this small book is my encouragement for you to do the same.

So—regardless of what comes your way each day, trust in God's love for you.

Having a good day? Thank God for it.

Struggling through a bad day? Invite God into it.

Just another "ordinary" day? Find God in it.

And—every day—praise God, for life is a gift never to be wasted.

Just tweet others as you wish to be tweeted.

All for her Son,

Mark Hart

Feast of St. John Chrysostom

. . . . # . . . .

Everything we have—every blessing, every talent—is a gift from
our Father. The only thing that's all ours is our sin. #GodisLove

. . . . # . . . .

God will put someone in your path today who doesn't necessarily
need you...but who desperately needs Christ in you. #beprepared
#love

. . . . # . . . .

If the people of Nazareth taught us anything, it's that God could
be right in front of you and you might not even recognize Him.
#Eucharist

. . . . # . . . .

.... # ....

Christianity is not about being a "nice" person; it's about becoming a new person (Gal 2:20).

.... # ....

This is one of the greatest misunderstandings about Christianity in the modern age. Christianity is not about behavior modification or general human platitudes. Christianity is a death to pride, selfishness, and the world. It is becoming a "little Christ" and living in a selfless way—living for others.

.... # ....

The joy of "knowing Christ" is less about us knowing Him than it is realizing (and rejoicing) that He knows, loves, and saves us (Lk 10:20-21).

.... # ....

. . . . # . . . .

My middle daughter—the dancing machine—just taught me how to do a "coffee grinder." I think I just ruptured my spleen.

. . . . # . . . .

I love You, Lord. #prayitdaily #idareyou

. . . . # . . . .

If you want to live as a Christian, get comfortable with being uncomfortable.

. . . . # . . . .

St. Peter felt the need to complain before doing what the Lord asked (Lk 5:5). Wow, I'm more saintly than I originally thought. #humbling

. . . . # . . . .

.... # ....

Consider the manger, the cross, the empty tomb...most of God's greatest gifts involve some suffering, sacrifice, or a sense of loss.

.... # ....

How comforting that even in those dark nights of the soul, the sanctuary candle is still burning brightly. #truepresence

.... # ....

Just keep smiling...just keep smiling...this guy's lucky I'm a Christian...just keep smiling...

.... # ....

Living the Christian life doesn't mean that nothing bothers you. If anything, you have an even more heightened awareness of sin—yours and others—but you refuse to be mastered by it.

.... # ....

.... # ....

God didn't give us The Ten "Suggestions" (Ex 20:1-17).

.... # ....

Those souls who pick and choose which commandments they follow (i.e., missing Mass on Sundays) are not following the Lord, but themselves. God loves us too much to play word games. He gives us the Commandments for our own good, to save us from ourselves.

.... # ....

Doubting God's love for you or whether God will provide for you (Gn 3:4-5)? Don't. Tell the devil to go to hell...that's where he belongs.

.... # ....

. . . . # . . . .

Never quite understood the whole "barbed wire" tattoo thing.
When that guy's eighty years old the barbed wire's gonna look like
a weathered picket fence.

. . . . # . . . .

Our salvation may have cost us nothing, but true discipleship
costs us everything. (1 Cor 6:20; Lk 9:23)

. . . . # . . . .

Modern culture isn't in bad shape because of what it consumes.
Modern culture is in bad shape because it's so consumed with self.

. . . . # . . . .

. . . . # . . . .

"Tolerance" does not render objective truth untrue. The Gospel is not politically correct. Political correctness crucifies Truth.

. . . . # . . . .

Some are labeled "bigots" for speaking difficult Gospel truths. The fact is that not to share truth is the sin. Christ is clear: "When your brother sins, rebuke him and when he repents, forgive him" (Luke 17:3).

. . . . # . . . .

God laughs and weeps...He even whistles (Ps 2:4; Jn 11:35; Is 5:26). He knows what it is to be human & can handle anything you throw at Him.

. . . . # . . . .

. . . . # . . . .

Today, God intends to make you a great saint...if you let Him.
Don't run. Don't squirm. Just lean into grace.

. . . . # . . . .

You know the funny thing about sin? God doesn't (Lk 12:4-5;
Rom 6:23).

. . . . # . . . .

Wow! Apparently Gloria Estefan was right...this morning the
rhythm did, indeed, get me.

. . . . # . . . .

. . . . # . . . .

Twitter's great for figuring out which souls following you have a sense of humor and which had a humor-ectomy at some point. #prayforthem

. . . . # . . . .

SEX! Okay, now that I have your attention...God loves you. Never. forget. it. #JesusChristisLord

. . . . # . . . .

In the Lord's Prayer, Jesus offers more than God's personal email or private cell number—He offers us a heart transplant. #PerfectPrayer

. . . . # . . . .

.... # ....

If God did everything my way—according to my plans—
well then He really wouldn't be God. #Trust

.... # ....

*Many struggle with this reality. For
countless souls, God is more of a genie
who is supposed to do their bidding or a
lucky rabbit's foot you go to when in need.
Unless we submit to God's authority, He
really isn't God, is He?*

.... # ....

Lord, we both know that I need you more than You need me.
So, thank You for the blood and the water. #Savior

.... # ....

. . . . # . . . .

Life's too short not to tell the people you love how you feel. Say it...and say it often. Oh, and start with God—1 John 4:19.

. . . . # . . . .

If you refuse to change, what are you giving the Lord permission to do, really?

. . . . # . . . .

For Christians the question isn't whether or not God exists or if Christ is Lord—the question is how deeply those truths change your life.

. . . . # . . . .

. . . . # . . . .

What did all the saints have in common? They feared sin more than even physical death. Sin is the worst kind of death (Rom 6:23).

. . . . # . . . .

Living out virtue often feels like you're doing a 100-yard dash... in a 90-yard gym. Run anyway.

. . . . # . . . .

Oh, how thunderous the applause must be in heaven, all those times we are mocked on earth...for the sake of His Name (Mt 5:11-12).

. . . . # . . . .

.... # ....

No sin is bigger than mercy. No sin. #DivineMercy

.... # ....

*In Scripture when Christ tells us about
"the unforgivable sin," it means the sin we
don't ask forgiveness for, that pride is the
sin against the Holy Spirit, not allowing
God to forgive you (Mark 3:29).*

.... # ....

Sunday doesn't just prepare us for the week ahead—
it prepares us for eternity. #tasteofHeaven

.... # ....

If your words are not better than silence...be silent. #virtue

.... # ....

.... # ....

It breaks my heart when couples focus more on being wed than being married. Two becoming one doesn't happen without work, humility & sacrifice.

.... # ....

I'm going to encourage my cab driver to think about going to seminary...I've never had a person get me to pray so much.

.... # ....

Authentic Christianity is a roller-coaster ride, not a merry-go-round. Buckle up and throw your arms in the air. #Godisincontrol

.... # ....

God loves us too much to pretend our sin isn't there. Sin is a cancer and Christ the surgeon. True prayer signs the consent form.

.... # ....

.... # ....

True friends are the people who ask how you are doing and then wait—genuinely wanting to hear your answer.

.... # ....

Your worth lies in who you are—and in Whose you are— not in what you do (Lk 10:20).

.... # ....

Prayer doesn't make God love you more. Sin doesn't make God love you less. His love is not based on our actions. Prayer improves our ability to receive God's love. Sin severs the relationship. Prayer is a gift.

.... # ....

.... # ....

Scripture says God didn't give the ostrich wisdom but speed (Job 39:13-18). I think the guy in front of me on the freeway was part ostrich.

.... # ....

Don't wear a cross around your neck if all you're going to do is complain about the one on your back.

.... # ....

Well, I'm off to pay for my dentist's summer vacation (Job 19:20). #RedemptiveSuffering

.... # ....

. . . . # . . . .

Yes, sometimes God does work in mysterious ways—but often times He is really, really obvious (Dt 30:11).

. . . . # . . . .

We often like to claim we don't know what God wants when, in reality, we do and we just don't like His answer to our question.

. . . . # . . . .

A rib...loaves and fish...some spit....
God can do a lot with very little.

. . . . # . . . .

By God's grace we can overcome all fears (2 Cor 12:9).
Edison was afraid of the dark. Walt Disney was afraid of mice.
#irony #inspiration

. . . . # . . . .

.... # ....

"Daddy, will I get hurt if I jump off the roof?" Me: "We both will...you by the ground & me by your mother. So don't even think about it."

.... # ....

Let us never forget that "keeping the Sabbath holy" is more than just going to Church. Rest. Pray. Be present to family. Pray. Laugh. Pray.

.... # ....

God truly is the funniest person I know.

.... # ....

I believe that standing ovations are 95% peer pressure.

.... # ....

.... # ....

God already knows what you need; now He just wants to hear you say it. #prayer

.... # ....

Why can't the more challenging questions hit us when we're sixteen...and know everything? #youthministry

.... # ....

Too many walk aimlessly through the day—Christians cannot. Jesus "went about doing good" (Acts 10:38). Christianity is intentional.

.... # ....

The only thing deadlier than sin is the denial of it.

.... # ....

.... # ....

If the person who says they love you is unwilling to sacrifice for you...it ain't love (Jn 15:13; Eph 5:25).

.... # ....

Prayer isn't about getting what we want, but about becoming what God wants us to be (ruminating on James 4:8).

.... # ....

At the Last Supper, the other 11 called Him "Lord" but the Iscariot did not. Evil could not utter such a term of humility (Mt 26:21-25).

.... # ....

It's essential to really read the Scriptures, especially those stories you have heard so many times before. Love is in the details.

.... # ....

.... # ....

The term "excruciating" literally means "out of the cross."
#GoodFriday

.... # ....

Countless souls wait for a miracle before they will bow to Christ.
The "good" thief witnessed no miracle, he witnessed only #Mercy
(Lk 23).

.... # ....

"The people hung upon His words" (Lk 19:48)—that is, until they
hung Him on a cross. Admiration is fleeting. Love is eternal.

.... # ....

The miracle of Good Friday is that there was no miracle.
Legions of angels stood—with swords sheathed—
watching as the Son took our place.

.... # ....

.... # ....

Using death to defeat death...wow. No way the devil saw that one coming. God has style (1 Cor 15:21).

.... # ....

If Jesus didn't rise, an even greater miracle happened: 12 relatively uneducated guys changed the world & were martyred
to protect a lie.

.... # ....

The Resurrection is neither optimism nor idealism; it is truth. Atheism proclaims the tomb is full; Christians know it is empty.
#Easter!

.... # ....

Trying to kiss my wife good-bye while she was mid-run on the treadmill gave me an odd new appreciation for the challenges of hamster romance.

.... # ....

.... # ....

It's one of the greatest comforts of working in ministry: the unspoken certitude that your spouse did not marry you for your money. :)

.... # ....

Silly Lazarus, tombs are for dead people (Jn 11:1-45).
#Resurrection

.... # ....

Sssshhh. God is speaking. #Listen

.... # ....

My 5-yr-old: "Daddy, what do I tell a boy who says he wants to marry me?" Me: "First he has to work for me 14 years without pay" (Gn 29).

.... # ....

.... # ....

Even God's spit is more powerful than medicine (Jn 9:1-41).
#DivineOptometrist

.... # ....

*Some modern scholars like to say that
Christ didn't really work miracles, that
the accounts are just literary devices.
Don't listen to them. Trust in the saints,
not the scholars. Trust in the Holy Spirit.*

.... # ....

"Look, you're beautiful but I really like this place...so I'm gonna
pass on the fruit." #stuffAdamshouldhavesaid

.... # ....

24

. . . . # . . . .

Even when skies are grey and clouds heavy with tears, the sun
rises. So to with our souls, burdened by life's sins & still He rises.
#Sabbath

. . . . # . . . .

How boring life would be if God did things our way.
1 John 4:19. That's why.

. . . . # . . . .

Silence is the quickest, most prayerful way to find out what we
really believe about God. Prayer is not a monologue.

. . . . # . . . .

*Many of us want to know why we don't
"hear" God when we pray. Few of us shut
up long enough to really listen.*

. . . . # . . . .

. . . . # . . . .

Those who find obedience demeaning ought to consider the most obedient person in history (Jn 5:30). #JesusChrist

. . . . # . . . .

There's a difference between being uncomfortable with change and unwilling to change. Christianity is all about change...not comfort.

. . . . # . . . .

Maybe if we said that sin causes cancer, people would take it more seriously (Rom 6:23). #deadlierthanevencancer

. . . . # . . . .

Authentic prayer is a bold invitation—a heartfelt submission, begging the Holy Spirit to ruin your best-laid plans.

. . . . # . . . .

.... # ....

An attorney for the 3 Pigs maintains that his clients did not knowingly plagiarize Scripture (Mt 7:24-27) in the telling of "their tale."

.... # ....

A husband I met tried to justify his "harmless" porn addiction by telling me that it keeps him faithful to his wife. Um... #pornISadultery

.... # ....

God doesn't desire our worship because He is egocentric... He desires it because we are. #perspective #Divineaid

.... # ....

Run all you want...God runs faster. We are such silly sheep (Mt 18:12).

.... # ....

.... # ....

I submit one of the quickest ways to lower anxiety in your day is to forbid others from using CAPS LOCK or multiple !!s in their emails.

.... # ....

In my prayer this morning I actually said, "Lord, I talk too much when I pray." #irony I think I even heard God laugh.

.... # ....

A nervous teen (in very baggy pants): "Mark, any words of wisdom before my date tonight?" Me: "Wear a belt... and keep wearin' it" (2 Tim 2:22).

.... # ....

If you want to love like Christ you need to walk the extra mile...& the one after that...& the one after that...(Mt 10:38) #yougettheidea

.... # ....

. . . . # . . . .

Valentine's Day should not be as much a quest for a what (love) as it should be for a Who (Love)—1 John 4:19.

. . . . # . . . .

Note to self: if you want to love God better...hate sin more. Heaven is an invitation. Hell is a decision.

. . . . # . . . .

There is a popular misconception that God "sends us to hell." In reality, sin is our rejection of God's invitation to heaven. God honors our free will when we reject His love (sin), and allows us to live eternally without Him (hell) just as we sought to live without Him on earth.

. . . . # . . . .

.... # ....

Sowing is not nearly as much fun as reaping, but both are
necessary for the kingdom (Eccl 3:2).

.... # ....

Whenever I get an angry email, I try to remember the time those in
Nazareth wanted to throw Jesus off a cliff (Lk 4:29)...
and I feel better.

.... # ....

God can live without you...He just doesn't want to (Col 1:22).

.... # ....

A prayer is the greatest gift, expression of love or act of service
you can render another soul.

.... # ....

· · · · · · · · · · · · · · · · # · · · · · · · · · · · · · · · · ·

Dorothy had a brick road. Hansel and Gretel had bread crumbs.
We have the Holy Spirit. We win. #FF #FollowGodtoGod

· · · · · · · · · · · · · · · · # · · · · · · · · · · · · · · · · ·

I'll bet—in retrospect—that Jack (& Jill) would have opted for
dehydration over a cerebral hemorrhage. #H2Ohno

· · · · · · · · · · · · · · · · # · · · · · · · · · · · · · · · · ·

It's pretty sad that when people see a guy buying flowers, they
assume he's in trouble. #ijustlovemywife

· · · · · · · · · · · · · · · · # · · · · · · · · · · · · · · · · ·

The soldiers treated God like a dog (Jn 18:12) - and two thousand
years later, millions still do. #spirituallybackward

· · · · · · · · · · · · · · · · # · · · · · · · · · · · · · · · · ·

.... # ....

Save your favors...God wants your heart and won't stop until you place it in His nail-scarred hands.

.... # ....

You can usually tell by the look on someone's face if they woke up counting their problems or their blessings (Jas 1:17).

.... # ....

If I accomplish nothing on my "to do" list today, but I still make time for prayer—"to be" with my Father—I am successful. #perspective

.... # ....

In prayer I find myself pondering the Magi's trip home—their bags and boxes empty but their hearts quite full (Mt 2:12). #foreverchanged

.... # ....

.... # ....

Love is always on a mission (Jn 10:10; 1 Jn 4:9-12).

.... # ....

We are called to love God and one another.
That is our primary vocation. The reason
we rise in the morning and the purpose of
our life on earth is to learn how to receive
God's love and then share it. God's gift of
life to you each morning is a sign that He
has a mission for you that day.

.... # ....

Advent might be the only time in my life
that I don't mind waiting.

.... # ....

.... # ....

I've met knowledgeable people who don't know God but have yet
to meet a truly wise person who does not.

.... # ....

God's has great plans for you today, creative and unexpected
means by which He will make you a saint. He needs only your
joyful submission.

.... # ....

Married couples, may we never forget that when attacks come—
the grace of the sacrament is eternally stronger than we are.

.... # ....

Truly contemplative prayer is when you can hear God exhale.
#peace

.... # ....

.... # ....

We must not become so preoccupied looking for "major" miracles that we miss all the daily ones.

.... # ....

"Thy Kingdom come" means "My Kingdom go." #ChristtheKing

.... # ....

Sunday worship is not merely about devotion—it's about reception. The Sabbath rest is grace in action.

.... # ....

If we all entered into the Sabbath beyond "just going to Church," the week that follows would look very different. It wouldn't hurt our stress level, either.

.... # ....

.... # ....

There's often a difference between "taking" your problems to the Lord and giving your problems to the Lord. #trustinGod

.... # ....

Trying to explain to my 2-yr-old that Joseph from Genesis isn't the same as St. Joseph. She's worried that Jesus had mean uncles. #wow

.... # ....

It's right when you're "convinced" that God hasn't heard your prayers...when He shows you—once again—how wrong you are.

.... # ....

"This man receives sinners and eats with them" (Lk 15:2). Yes. He. Does. At every single Mass.

.... # ....

.... # ....

People with a lot of theological study and no prayer life are dangerous...and not in a good way.

.... # ....

Your greatest joy should not come from all you do in His Name, but from the fact that He knows your name (Lk 10:20).

.... # ....

Eye hath not seen and ear hath not heard what happens when a 2-yr.-old discovers "Pixy Stix" for the first time.

.... # ....

Love rarely comes in the form, the manner, or the person we're expecting (Lk 1:26; Mt 1:20; Lk 2:12).

.... # ....

.... # ....

Worshipping Jesus transfigured is a whole lot easier and more comfortable than worshipping Jesus disfigured. #passion #perspective

.... # ....

You can tell a great deal about a person's Christianity by the way they treat their waiter or waitress (Lk 22:27).

.... # ....

Watching the sunrise is always a godly encounter, but there's something about a Sunday sunrise that always hits me deeper. #Resurrection

.... # ....

He is the door not the doormat. He is merciful not weak. He is the way not a way. He is Love. He is Lord. He is Jesus.

.... # ....

.... # ....

It is so beautifully ironic that St. Francis—the great lover of animals—is now a pigeon's target in countless yards. #humility

.... # ....

When my wife tells me that I'm handsome, my natural response is, "Thanks honey...how much is this going to cost?" #suburbanwisdom

.... # ....

Sharing Christ's light with others requires both mercy and patience. Hearts blinded by evil's lies require time to dilate.

.... # ....

There are 590 words in Obadiah.
#thingsyoucansaytoendaconversation

.... # ....

.... # ....

If more husbands & fathers would put as much energy into their marriages & families as they do their jobs, the world would change.

.... # ....

Sometimes we forget that sin really is optional.

.... # ....

A sleeping child's exhale is one of the greatest incarnations of God's gentleness.

.... # ....

Eye contact is more than a polite gesture - it is a simple yet meaningful acknowledgement of Christ in the other.

.... # ....

.... # ....

The devil doesn't sit idly by while you seek God. If you're pursuing Christ, the enemy is pursuing you (Rom 7:21; 1 Pet 5:8).

.... # ....

The first mistake most Christians make is forgetting that they are embroiled in a war for souls. Your life is taking place on a battlefield. The enemy is real, and the sooner we realize that and proactively do something about it, the better off we and our families will be.

.... # ....

Our Sabbath practices reveal which Trinity we truly worship: Father, Son & Spirit...or me, myself & I.

.... # ....

.... # ....

We must constantly discern our struggles and where they come
from. God humbles, the devil humiliates.

.... # ....

Fish swim. Birds fly. We give glory to God by doing what we are
designed to do (1 Jn 4:7-8).

.... # ....

Gift bags are a socially acceptable celebration of laziness. I salute
the man who invented them. Oh yes, it had to be a man.

.... # ....

I advocate for every Church to have a lost & found...too many
Christians have misplaced their sense of humor (Ps 2:4).

.... # ....

.... # ....

I wonder if Pinocchio ever considered wearing
fire-retardant pants.

.... # ....

*Ever notice all the similarities between
Pinocchio and Jonah? Think about it.*

.... # ....

It's funny how the closer you get to God, the more you realize
how far you are from Him.

.... # ....

.... # ....

It's sad how modern culture perverts truth until it sounds
like absurdity and obscenity. Remember Gn 3:4-5.
#nothinghaschanged

.... # ....

Just turn on the nightly news for examples
of this truth.

.... # ....

Too often we believe that God's miracles are rare when, in truth,
they are constant. God is working miracles today. #eyestosee

.... # ....

Watching a guy who's bad at flirting is like driving by an accident
scene: you don't want to look, but you just have to...

.... # ....

.... # ....

Jesus said that no one has to follow Him...unless they want to live
(Jn 6:57-58; Lk 10:28; Jn 10:10). #choices

.... # ....

God opens doors that no one can close. So when God closes
doors, don't shove your foot in to stop it (Prov. 3:5-6). #trust

.... # ....

I'll bet if "Keep holy the Sabbath" instead read "I command you
to take a nap on Sunday"—more Christians would obey it.

.... # ....

The funny thing about the boy who gave away his loaves & fish is
that he, too, ended the day with a full stomach. #sacrificeisGodly

.... # ....

.... # ....

Remember that line in the gospel where Jesus says, "Hey, forget what I said...just do it your way"? Me, neither.

.... # ....

"Shake well before using" was God's idea (Heb 12:26-28). The devil is not afraid of you, but he is petrified of Christ in you.

.... # ....

Never forget that the devil and Christ are not equals. The devil is merely an angel. Jesus is God. St. Michael can handle the evil one. Invite St. Michael into your corner; pray his prayer daily.

.... # ....

God created the smile. People should use it more. #creationreflectsitsCreator

.... # ....

.... # ....

True holiness is not achieved by what we do, but by what we allow God to do in us.

.... # ....

Family is the most direct path God gives you to attain sainthood.

.... # ....

The concept of a "split plate charge" fascinates me...what a tremendous way to teach our children not to share.

.... # ....

Has your day thus far reflected a desire for heaven or earth?

.... # ....

.... # ....

Fatherhood: how God blesses you out of your selfishness and floods your soul with love, all while reminding you how little you know...

.... # ....

Holiness is not the achievement of the few but the call of the many...the call of us all, actually (1 Thes 4:3-4).

.... # ....

Still processing the past few days...beginning to think the beautiful mystery of many miracles is that they're not immediately discernible.

.... # ....

How easy it is in modern culture to cease praying but still "want" God—we forget, prayer IS our relationship with God.

.... # ....

.... # ....

I feel so spiritually immature some days. When Jesus passes me the cup and bids me to drink...I'm hoping it's a sippy cup.

.... # ....

Every night I learn more about true prayer—not from scholars or spiritual writers—but from my own children. #humbled

.... # ....

I can't understand the "language" coming out of the drive-thru speaker. I don't blame the person...I blame Babel (Gn 11:7-9).

.... # ....

The road to heaven is narrow. The road to hell has an HOV lane (Mt 7:13-14).

.... # ....

.... # ....

If the Lord didn't want us to grow in patience, He would never have given us families. :)

.... # ....

Never once in Scripture does God say, "Don't call Me—I'll call you." #pray

.... # ....

To all the brave men and women who offered their lives so we could live in freedom...sincerely, "Thank you." #memorialday (Jn 15:13)

.... # ....

Believe your beliefs. Doubt your doubts. Behold God's Mystery. #TrinitySunday

.... # ....

. . . . # . . . .

Oh, how much holier the world would be if more people invoked
their right to remain silent (Prv 17:28).

. . . . # . . . .

We can't experience all that heaven has to offer until we renounce
all that the world offers in its place.

. . . . # . . . .

If I say I believe in the Scriptures, that means I believe in all they
convey—and that means, first, that I have to believe God loves
me.

. . . . # . . . .

The atheist barista (who's obsessed with astrology) asked
me, "So, what's your sign?" Me: "The sign of the cross."
#ithinkshespitinmycoffee

. . . . # . . . .

.... # ....

"Anti-Christian" people don't do nearly as much damage to Christ's Church as joyless Christians do.

.... # ....

Lord, save me today from any of your children who lack a sense of humor.

.... # ....

My 4-yr-old: "Daddy, has Dr. Seuss sold more books than you?" Me: "Yes, a LOT more." Her: "Maybe you should start making yours rhyme."

.... # ....

Never complain about growing old...some never have the privilege.

.... # ....

.... # ....

You can't hook a U-Haul up to a hearse (Mt 16:26).
#liveforheaven

.... # ....

People working in ministry should be encouraged to take more naps. St. Joseph did his best work asleep (Mt 1:20; 2:12, 19).

.... # ....

You'll notice that all three times when the angel comes to St. Joseph, he is sleeping. Possibly the news was more than he could handle awake. Or maybe God is encouraging me to rest more. (Note: this does not empower sleeping during the homily.)

.... # ....

. . . . # . . . .

When you are under attack - call in reinforcements. Intercessory
prayer is a gift...that works (1 Tm 2:1-4).

. . . . # . . . .

"Love one another" (Jn 13:35). No command is simpler; no
command more difficult.

. . . . # . . . .

A Christian who lacks joy is like a vegetarian who works as a
butcher or an animal-rights activist wearing mink. #contradiction

. . . . # . . . .

It always feels weird to me when someone tells me how much
they've grown in humility.

. . . . # . . . .

. . . . # . . . .

Note to self: If you can't hear God when you pray...shut up.

. . . . # . . . .

God is love (1 Jn 4:8). God is life (Jn 10:10). So, without love (God), we are not really living, only breathing.

. . . . # . . . .

It is a great tragedy to go an entire day without laughter. It's a greater tragedy, still, to go a whole day without prayer.

. . . . # . . . .

Today offers limitless possibilities for holiness. Lean into His grace. The only thing keeping us from sainthood is ourselves.

. . . . # . . . .

.... # ....

How can we possibly trust God in our death if we refuse to trust Him with our lives? Believe Prv 3:5-6.

.... # ....

Countless souls choose not to honor Christ—in their behavior, works or speech—while alive, yet magically expect Him to honor them upon their death. Scripture confirms that's not a good idea. Don't wait. Go to God today.

.... # ....

Prayer is where the cross changes shoulders.

.... # ....

.... # ....

It's comforting to know that no matter how many songs or analogies we come up with to describe God's grace, we're still not even close.

.... # ....

My godson: "What happens when I receive the Holy Spirit?"
Me: "You become one of God's Jedi."
Him: "Ya, that's pretty much what I figured."

.... # ....

"And Mary set out...in HASTE" (Lk 1:39). The good news of Christ carries with it a joyful urgency. It must be shared.

.... # ....

No one would have blamed the apostles if they had just stuck with fishing...but no one would have remembered them, either.

.... # ....

.... # ....

If today you "kill somebody with kindness" be sure to draw a
smiley face on the chalk outline. Remember Romans 12:10.

.... # ....

I love when people ask for permission to ask a stupid question.
Lent ought to reveal the dehydration of our souls (Jn 7:37).

.... # ....

God doesn't abandon the stubborn; He challenges them.
You're not the first to wrestle with God (Gn 32:24-25).

.... # ....

If you want to be truly happy, seek first to be truly holy
(Jer 15:16; Mt 6:33).

.... # ....

.... # ....

The Word of God is meant to be proclaimed in word and deed, not merely thought and theory (2 Tm 4:2; Col 3:16; Jas 2:24).

.... # ....

It's #datenight with my wife. She looks like a million dollars. Good thing I'm not British—I'd hate to say a million pounds.

.... # ....

My 2-yr-old fell asleep in my arms tonight. Her exhale, a rhythmic prayer echoing God's love. He is a God of life (Jn 10:10).

.... # ....

Song of Songs may be "romantic" but, guys, don't quote it. No woman wants her hair compared to a flock of goats (4:1) or her teeth to ewes (4:2).

.... # ....

.... # ....

Lord, I don't ask for much...but I pray you will send a drought—
of biblical proportions —on Farmville.

.... # ....

God desires our worship, that's why He renders us capable of it.
"You've changed" is a great affirmation for a Christian to receive.
When new life in Christ vanquishes our former self, heaven
applauds.

.... # ....

*Often we become annoyed when someone
says such a thing. The truth is that if you're
living in such a way that people notice a
difference in you, you're doing something
right! Christianity is about becoming a
new creation, not a "better version" of
your old self.*

.... # ....

.... # ....

God's love is patient, kind, unconditional AND powerful. We must never confuse God's mercy with weakness.

.... # ....

Countless desire a Godly love in their dating relationships but, sadly, a Godly love is the first thing many forfeit in the process.

.... # ....

A healthy, holy marriage is not about finding the right person— it's about becoming the right person (Gal 2:20).

.... # ....

Christians shouldn't whine. Christ called us to be the "salt of the earth" (Mt 5:13), yes, but not the Veruca Salt. #OompaLoompadobadeedont

.... # ....

.... # ....

If God had given us 15 Commandments, I feel pretty confident that Number Eleven would have said, "Thou shalt not touch another man's fries."

.... # ....

The man who built that manger had a purpose in mind...God had another. You'll never know how far reaching God's plan is for your work.

.... # ....

The baby's exhale, the parents' adoring stare, the angelic host bowing in worship...an overenthusiastic percussionist offering a drum solo. #parumpumpumpum

.... # ....

Any parent of a newborn can understand the humor in this beautiful song.

.... # ....

.... # ....

BREAKING: Bethlehem PD has apprehended a local drummer for disturbing the peace. The suspect's only comment was, "Come, they told me."

.... # ....

Christ multiplied the loaves, but He allowed apostles to distribute it. God's glory is revealed not merely in the gift, but in the giving.

.... # ....

Oh, how beautiful life would be if we were all as forgiving as our dogs.

.... # ....

Due to tax challenges, the Magi—if American—would be forced to offer the Christ child gifts of aluminum, cloves, and some aspartame.

.... # ....

.... # ....

My daughter: "Isn't it cool that Mary wrapped the world's first Christmas presents? It's like the swaddling clothes were the gift wrap!"

.... # ....

After his success rubbing the lamp, Aladdin spent the next several years massaging other household appliances to no avail. #therestofthestory

.... # ....

Marriage isn't about finding someone you can "live with," but about celebrating someone you cannot live without.

.... # ....

Luke 1:28—it's the only time in Scripture that an angel addresses someone by a title rather than a name. #worthyofreflection #holyMary

.... # ....

.... # ....

Love may be patient but Love doesn't just sit & wait.
Love pursues. How overwhelming to realize that God (Love) is
always in pursuit of us.

.... # ....

Seek God's will...nothing more, nothing less, nothing else.

.... # ....

God's favor rests upon those who are of one mind and heart...His.

.... # ....

There's a difference between being uncomfortable with change and
unwilling to change. Christianity is all about change...not comfort.

.... # ....

. . . . # . . . .

The truest friends are usually the ones telling you what you don't want to hear (Sir 6:14).

. . . . # . . . .

You don't become a saint by comparing yourself to a sinner.

. . . . # . . . .

It's easy to feel good about yourself when you compare your behavior and life to those more sinful than yourself. Aim higher.

. . . . # . . . .

What annoys us most in other people is often times the same area God wants to grow us in ourselves. #Heisfunnythatway

. . . . # . . . .

. . . . # . . . .

True holiness is not achieved by what we do, but by what we allow God to do in us.

. . . . # . . . .

Children: God's most beautiful alarm clocks (Ps 127:3).

. . . . # . . . .

Lord, thank you for car alarms, without which many of your overtired children could never find their automobiles in a parking garage.

. . . . # . . . .

God doesn't work off of our timetables. His timing is perfect (Eccl 3:1; Gal 4:4). Be patient and trust Him.

. . . . # . . . .

.... # ....

Lord Jesus, I give you permission to remove anything and anyone from my life that will keep me from sainthood...that will keep me from You.

.... # ....

This is a prayer I dare you to pray daily.
It has upended my life in a beautiful way.
It's scary and enlivening at the same time.
Pray it...and then keep praying it.

.... # ....

Notes to self: Don't pretend to be a saint—intend to be one. Bend your knees but never your morals.

.... # ....

.... # ....

If true love were only about feelings, Jesus would have been hugged to death for our redemption. Thank God for His cross this and every day.

.... # ....

Rules for today: 1. Pray. 2. Laugh. 3. Repeat. The only reason to take this life too seriously is if it's your only one.

.... # ....

If it had said, "...part of your heart, some of your soul, most of your mind and a fraction of your strength," I'd be looking good right now.

.... # ....

Those souls empowered with the privilege of preaching and teaching the faith have an enormous responsibility. Prayer must precede all else.

.... # ....

.... # ....

Real men don't need mistletoe.

.... # ....

I'm embarrassed it's taken me this long to say this publicly, but here goes..."Thank You, God, for peanut butter. Amen." #itsthelittlethings

.... # ....

The devil loves complacency.

.... # ....

Sometimes evil breathes simply in our doing nothing when called to speak or to act. As Edmund Burke reminded us, "All that is necessary for the triumph of evil is that good men do nothing."

.... # ....

.... # ....

Ever doubt that God answers your prayers? Pray (sincerely) for humility...and watch what happens.

.... # ....

Friday and Saturday nights have a funny way of revealing what we really believe on Sunday mornings.

.... # ....

Prayer is one of the greatest times to invoke your right to remain silent. #listen

.... # ....

"Pay attention to what I am telling you..."—Jesus (Lk 9:44) #simple #truth

.... # ....

.... # ....

"Daddy, why did Jesus die?" Me: " He died for you." Her: "I don't get it." Me: "Most people don't." #lovehurts

.... # ....

God is still working miracles.

.... # ....

Playing board games with my daughters. At what point in history did "cheaters" begin getting associated with eating pumpkin?

.... # ....

Holy Week reminds us that while sometimes grace comes gently, it often comes painfully and, sometimes, grace comes violently.

.... # ....

.... # ....

Jesus wasn't mounted to the wood. Christ, our Savior, victoriously mounted the Cross that day. #GoodFriday

.... # ....

Darkness enveloped Gethsemane that night, but the embers of the Holy Spirit's fire burned brightly beneath the floorboards of the Upper Room

.... # ....

Gethsemane—literally translated—means "the place of crushing."

.... # ....

Peter's response to the washing of feet reminds us that we need submission to God's cleansing grace. Freedom through submission (Jn 13:8-9).

.... # ....

.... # ....

Every modern houseboat designer and manufacturer owes Noah a fat royalty. #reparationsofBiblicalproportions

.... # ....

Fatherhood is more than just a responsibility or a blessing...it is a privilege. Thank You, Lord.

.... # ....

It's always easier to look at oneself in the mirror after sin has closed the blinds to the room (1 Cor 13:11-12; Jas 1:23-25).

.... # ....

Life was a lot more adventurous before caller I.D.

.... # ....

.... # ....

Preaching Christ's truth always bears fruit... Of course, some people will probably end up wanting to throw that fruit at you (Mt 5:10-12).

.... # ....

Temptations most often enter through those doors we deliberately leave open. Self-awareness is the key to holiness.

.... # ....

During breakfast my daughter asked me if Noah found a pot of gold at the end of God's rainbow. I'm still laughing about it.

.... # ....

. . . . # . . . .

Christ is the head, Mary the neck and we the body.

. . . . # . . . .

Many Christians are confused as to why Catholics honor Mary the way that we do. She is different, however. She was set apart. One of the greatest things a Christian can do is to contemplate the life of Christ through Mary's eyes. As we see in sacred Scripture, she pondered things "in her heart" (Luke 2:19).

. . . . # . . . .

Ah, nothing says morning like sunlight creeping through the shades, the smell of fresh coffee brewing and a 4-yr-old's foot to your groin.

. . . . # . . . .

. . . . # . . . .

Christ always calls us to life and constantly to greater joy, but rarely does He call us to comfort.

. . . . # . . . .

Seeking words of wisdom? Let it be...done unto me according to Thy word (Lk 1:38).

. . . . # . . . .

Parenthood doesn't just "benefit" from God's grace...it requires it. Parenthood without grace is just babysitting kids (who probably look like you).

. . . . # . . . .

If personal holiness is not the primary goal of someone working in ministry then they need to step out of it (Mt 6:33). Prayer first.

. . . . # . . . .

.... # ....

His grace is strong enough to forever change you, if you are humble enough to let Him (2 Cor 12:9).

.... # ....

Reconciliation is the fastest way to change your life.

.... # ....

Confession is one of the greatest gifts Christ gave to His Church. The sacrament of penance offers you grace that is incomparable in your quest for sanctity.

.... # ....

God doesn't need your favors. He desires your joyful obedience.

.... # ....

. . . . # . . . .

Me: "Get in the bath. Yes, Jesus bathed, too. Get in the bath.
I just know. Get in the bath. Um, the River Jordan.
Now, get in the bath."

. . . . # . . . .

Remember, God doesn't just love you...He likes you.

. . . . # . . . .

Life isn't about what you know. Life is about Who you know
(Jn 14:9-21).

. . . . # . . . .

Lord Jesus, thank you for shins—without which many of your
children could never find furniture in the dark.

. . . . # . . . .

.... # ....

Don't be surprised when attacks come—if you're living for Christ they'll come constantly (Rom 7:21). It means you're doing it right.

.... # ....

Your Christianity is measured by how well you love those who can't stand you (Lk 6:32). Hmm.

.... # ....

Repentance makes the heart grow fonder...and holier.

.... # ....

Note to self: You're better off dealing with "an angry bear than a fool" (Prv 17:12). Wisdom says to let certain calls go to voice mail.

.... # ....

.... # ....

Never underestimate the power of a holy example (1 Pt 5:3).

.... # ....

To my daughters: "Do you think Jesus screamed & fought with other children over Silly Putty?" My 4-yr-old: "No...He probably multiplied it."

.... # ....

God will ultimately have His way. Our knees can buckle from stress or can kneel from reverence. To choose humility is to choose wisely.

.... # ....

My 4-yr-old: "People shouldn't put peanut butter with jelly. PB goes with chocolate...that's how God made it." #gospelaccordingtoreeses

.... # ....

.... # ....

Note to self: if you want to love God better...hate sin more.

.... # ....

Details matter. "Take up your cross DAILY and follow me"
(Lk 9:23). St. Luke is the only writer who adds "daily."
Love is in the details.

.... # ....

Prayer is the only thing that can increase the glory and majesty of
sunrise.

.... # ....

It's ironic how slow you feel on days that you fast.

.... # ....

.... # ....

If you're confused as to why God would die for you, you either need to rethink your vision of His mercy or of your own worth.

.... # ....

God is constantly looking past our unworthiness and reaffirming our worth.

.... # ....

The commandments are a gift, not a curse. Sin is less about breaking the rules and more about breaking the Father's heart.

.... # ....

Prayer should be more listening than speaking. God gave you two ears and one mouth...use them proportionately.

.... # ....

.... # ....

The Church needs more people willing to wash the feet (Jn 13:4-5) ...not just point out they're dirty or complain they smell.

.... # ....

Meek does not mean weak. Meekness requires true strength (Mt 5:5). True power is robed in humility.

.... # ....

I hear far more people discuss the presence of evil in their lives than they do the supreme power of grace. God is bigger than evil!

.... # ....

My kids asked why they have middle names. Me: "So you'll know when Mommy and Daddy are losing their patience."

.... # ....

.... # ....

My daughter's classmate called her "cutie pants."
This may be my last tweet as a free man.
Live out Mt 25:36—visiting hrs. are on Sat.

.... # ....

God said the people in Nineveh didn't know their right from their
left (Jonah 4:11). The guy who cut me off in traffic—
may be a Ninevite.

.... # ....

The God of the heavens loves you too much to share you with the
false gods of earth. He's beautifully jealous & He's unapologetic
about it.

.... # ....

Governments fail. Economies fail. Leaders fail. Athletes fail. Banks
fail. But love..."Love never fails" (1 Cor 13:8).

.... # ....

.... # ....

Counterfeit love costs little. True love costs you everything.

.... # ....

Praying Luke 5:18-20...it's the Bible's first "ceiling fan."

.... # ....

Parenthood isn't just about mothers and fathers having kids. It's about kids having mothers and fathers. #bepresent

.... # ....

. . . . # . . . .

Jesus doesn't need us—that's the bad news. Jesus does, however, WANT us...that's the great news (Mk 3:13).

. . . . # . . . .

We talk often about how we are God's "hands and feet," which is true. That being said, we can't fall into the trap of thinking God needs us like we need Him. He's God—which makes the reality that He wants to use us and be in relationship with us an even sweeter, more profound truth.

. . . . # . . . .

Life's too short not to jump in the puddles (Mk 10:15).

. . . . # . . . .

.... # ....

How beautiful that after 2,000 years, no one can outdo "God is love." It's the most perfectly concise, hopeful phrase in history (1 Jn 4:8).

.... # ....

Father, You are the Potter...I am the Play-Doh (Is 64:8).
Let's make a masterpiece.

.... # ....

Virtue isn't just revealed in the huge moments of life...
it's revealed at rush hour, with telemarketers, in long lines &
church parking lots.

.... # ....

.... # ....

Don't make Christ ride shotgun.

.... # ....

Is God in control of your life, or are you? Does He have your permission to take you where He wants to, or are you the control freak who wants Him in the car but won't let Him steer?

.... # ....

Contemplating Christ's cross: He is dying—literally—for you to know how much He loves you.

.... # ....

I just asked my wife to hand me my "Walkman." I was referring, though, to my iPod. Apparently, I'm trapped in 1985.

.... # ....

.... # ....

God is holding you in His heart, right at this very moment. It's a fact that can make you feel so small yet so big at the same time.

.... # ....

As I get older I've come to realize: The best way to "get even" with someone is to forgive—and then forget.

.... # ....

If you really want to change someone's life today, don't just pray for them...pray WITH them.

.... # ....

My 4-yr-old, looking at a picture of St. Patrick and fleeing snakes: "God should have sent St. Patrick to Eden." #creativeproblemsolving

.... # ....

.... # ....

It's hard to put your foot in your mouth...if it's shut. Silence can be powerful. Scripture doesn't record one word from St. Joseph.

.... # ....

"Trust in the Lord": Those 4 words are a challenge, an invitation, a divine plea and a command...and, still, I struggle.

.... # ....

Kids: "Daddy, we don't like watching you and Mommy kiss so much." Me: "Well, Mommy's gorgeous, so you better wear blindfolds 'til college."

.... # ....

Sin is even more deadly than cancer (Rom 6:23; Mt 18:8-9; Lk 12:4)...but sin has a cure. Christ is the cure (Col 1:14). #reconcile

.... # ....

.... # ....

Ponder Is 1:3 and Mk 15:27. Christ is flanked by the dirty and "lowly" at both birth and death. The manger's wood prefigures the cross.

.... # ....

Only in Isaiah are we given the typical nativity set (crèche) imagery of the ox and the ass. Those animals do not appear in Matthew or Luke's Gospel accounts of Christ's birth.

.... # ....

I have come to love it when people call me (or, more specifically, morality) "old-fashioned"...God is timeless and TRUTH isn't dated.

.... # ....

.... # ....

Mistaking me for an employee, a very rude shopper just asked me where to find "Scottish tape." I replied, "Glasgow?" She did not laugh.

.... # ....

Where we spend our money shows a lot about where we are with God.

.... # ....

Prayer: beautiful or burdensome, authentic or awful, helpful or hellish, intimate or intimidating—we are fickle, He's not. Lean into grace.

.... # ....

My daughter (going over spelling words): "Daddy, what does c-h-a-s-t-i-t-y spell?" Me: "Dating."

.... # ....

.... # ....

How fragrant the myrrh, how thick the cloud of incense,
how shiny the gold—all paling in comparison
to radiance in the manger.

.... # ....

Authority means "author's right." God is the author of life
(Acts 3:15)...and characters can't tell the author what to write.

.... # ....

Thank God for those He sends into your life who lack
a sense of humor...it makes you more appreciative
for those who have one.

.... # ....

*If you've never read Matthew 6:21, now's
the time.*

.... # ....

. . . . # . . . .

If you want something done right, you have to do it
yourself..."and the Word became flesh and dwelt
among us" (Jn 1:14).

. . . . # . . . .

Me: "WHY is the baby Jesus in Barbie's Corvette and not in the
manger?" My daughter: "Barbie was babysitting...
Mary was tired after the trip."

. . . . # . . . .

When it comes to our salvation, God doesn't take chances...
He gives them. #Advent demonstrates the fulfillment of God's
promises.

. . . . # . . . .

.... # ....

A broken heart is merely an empty manger. Invite the Virgin and
the carpenter to pray beside you. Invite the Savior to dwell there.
#hope

.... # ....

Enthusiasm is contagious—so is a lack of it. Joyless Christians are
a greater assault on the gospel than atheism (1 Pt 3:15).

.... # ....

Emmanuel means "God with us." Bethlehem = "house of bread"
(ponder John 6:51). "Noel" = Christmas (in French). Pa rum pum
pum pum = nothing.

.... # ....

Consider Mt 2:2: Faith is more than staring at the heavens hoping
God exists. True faith moves you...it calls you to worship.

.... # ....

.... # ....

A parent asked me today, "How do you get your children to pray in church?" My response? "Pray at home." #doasidonotjustasisay

.... # ....

To sin is human...to persist in sin is just stupid. #reconcilewithGod

.... # ....

To my 7-yr-old: "Ready for your spelling test?" "No, no I'm not." Me: "What are you gonna do?" Her (smiling), "Pray." #Christisourhope

.... # ....

The less people know, the more eager they seem to share it. Oh, Proverbs 17:28, you are #sotrue.

.... # ....

. . . . # . . . .

Morning Journal: My life—the wood. My sins—the nails. And there is my Savior, right in the middle of it all.

. . . . # . . . .

My body desires sleep. My mind is not allowing it. Counting sheep isn't working. I'll just keep talking to the Shepherd...

. . . . # . . . .

Smash the jar. Pour out the oil. Hold nothing back. Christ deserves your best this and every day (Mk 14:3). #allforJesus

. . . . # . . . .

.... # ....

I ran and God called. I ran and God pursued. I ran and God rescued. Yet, at times, I still run. He truly is my Shepherd (Jn 10:11).

.... # ....

Don't get down on yourself if you're not perfect in your walk. That's why God gives us confession. Ask God for the grace to improve and then set your mind to it. Conversion is an ongoing process.

.... # ....

Good liturgy illuminates the senses and enraptures the soul; it elicits a response.

.... # ....

.... # ....

Teacher: "If your daughter knew her spelling words as well as her Bible stories she'd get into Harvard." Me: "I'll settle for heaven."

.... # ....

Are you "overwhelmed by excessive sorrow" (2 Cor 2:7)? If so, run into the arms of "excessive Love" (see Lk 15:20).

.... # ....

If we who are Christian could even begin to fathom the depth and breadth of Baptism...the world would look very different.

.... # ....

Quantum physics, the designated hitter, guys who wear skinny jeans...just a few examples of #thingsthatdontmakesensetome

.... # ....

.... # ....

Great morning prayer is like marinating in the Holy Spirit.

.... # ....

Tied my 7-yr-old in the "Rock, Paper, Scissors" World Championships, so I introduced "Lava"...which beats everything. I won. #toocompetitive

.... # ....

Some people say, "If you trust in God's unconditional love, why do you need to pray?" A better ending is "why wouldn't you want to?"

.... # ....

Today our family is focusing on service (Mt 23:11). During it, two of our girls began fighting over who'd serve the other. #perfectirony

.... # ....

. . . . # . . . .

Reality television is devoid of many things...most notably: reality.
#iwouldratherreadleviticus

. . . . # . . . .

Things will never go wrong at the right time (Jas 1:2; Jn 16:33).
#leanintograce

. . . . # . . . .

Smile. God created the smile.
#heavenANDeartharefilledwithHisglory

. . . . # . . . .

.... # ....

God didn't give Adam & Eve the right to decide what was good and evil. He gave them the right to choose between good & evil. #objectivetruth

.... # ....

Our modern culture—constantly attempting to redefine God's truth and His natural law—needs to be reminded of this truth. Of course, many of those souls don't believe in the authority of God's Word, so prayer is your best initial approach.

.... # ....

The Tooth Fairy made yet another visit to our home last night. I'm turning into an ATM. It's like there is money in their mouths (Mt 17:27).

.... # ....

.... # ....

Without me, God is still God...but without God, I am nothing.

.... # ....

Zacchaeus climbed a tree. Peter walked on water. Magi traveled over 1000 miles—all just to see Him. A relationship takes effort. #pray

.... # ....

Some judge friendship by the number of friends they have...instead of by the number of friends they'd die for. #thedangeroffacebook

.... # ....

God doesn't just "have a plan" for our salvation—He became the plan (Phil 2:6-16). The path to heaven is the way of the cross.

.... # ....

.... # ....

Much of Satan's time is spent trying to make you remember what God has already forgotten. Reconcile, rejoice, and look forward.

.... # ....

God didn't give us the Ten Suggestions. Christ did not offer the Beatitudes a la carte. This life is all or nothing...

.... # ....

Holiness is a steep, jagged, and narrow path. Worldliness is subtle, smooth, and wide. For which do I hope and seek each day?

.... # ....

I am a Christian not because of what I do, but because of Whose I am.

.... # ....

. . . . # . . . .

Today, I proclaimed Jesus as Lord, quoted Scripture, and encouraged someone to eat fruit...of course, the devil did all those, too.

. . . . # . . . .

The willingness to destroy human life begins in the heart, not the mind. If the heart is hardened, the intellect is darkened.

. . . . # . . . .

Entering a sleeping baby's room requires the silent precision of a Navy SEAL Team. By God's grace I succeeded. I am a suburban ninja.

. . . . # . . . .

.... # ....

Imagine what God could do with you if you really trusted Him.
Lord, save me...from myself.

.... # ....

*Often when we pray "deliver us from
evil" during the Lord's Prayer, we are
thinking of the evil "out there" in the
world when, in reality, we should also be
considering the evil inclinations that come
from within us (Mark 7:21).*

.... # ....

My 7-yr-old: "Daddy, does God put our favorite color in our
mind or heart? Or is it up to us?" Aquinas would love her.
#raisingaphilosopher

.... # ....

.... # ....

Nowhere in Scripture is Jesus recorded as saying, "My Dad could beat up your dad." It was pretty much understood.

.... # ....

It's only in seeing and experiencing Christ that we can finally see our true self—just ask Peter (Lk 5:8).

.... # ....

If I were as good at praying as I am at not praying...I'd be really holy.

.... # ....

The Lord's invitation is not to control but to contribute...do you still want in?

.... # ....

. . . . # . . . .

I've noticed that no matter how busy people are...they can still find time to tell me how busy they are.

. . . . # . . . .

Faith does not contradict reason...faith exceeds reason.

. . . . # . . . .

Modern minds are often shocked to find out that the Catholic Church does not teach that Genesis 1–11 has to be necessarily believed as scientific truth. It's allegory. That being said, we are called to believe its truth about God as Creator of all, being made in His image, original sin, and its effects, etc. It's a love story, not a science textbook.

. . . . # . . . .

. . . . # . . . .

I'm convinced the only time Barbie is actually dressed
is in her original packaging. My girls are looking for
"church appropriate" attire.

. . . . # . . . .

Reveal to me, Lord, all of those blessings that I take for granted.

. . . . # . . . .

You might want to start a list...

. . . . # . . . .

Fatherhood's taught me when it's too quiet...my kids are usually
sinning. God the Father knows the same. Are you praying?

. . . . # . . . .

.... # ....

I don't struggle with sin...I'm great at sinning. It's the whole "living in grace" thing I stink at. Help me, Jesus.

.... # ....

Stress will either drive you crazy or drive you to your knees. It depends on who is in control of your life.

.... # ....

It's tough for God to take us by the hand when we won't stop clutching the hems and robes of our false gods.

.... # ....

Prudence isn't as much about finding the right answers as it is about asking the right questions.

.... # ....

.... # ....

An annoyed and joyless Christian is one of the devil's greatest billboards.

.... # ....

If joy really is a fruit of the Holy Spirit, shouldn't all Christians unleash it? As G. K. Chesterton quipped, "Angels can fly because they take themselves so lightly." Don't be so serious that others can't see the joy of Christ in you.

.... # ....

Screams rang out as my girls fought over an Ariel doll. Like Solomon, I proposed we cut it in half (1 Kgs 3), but they BOTH ran for scissors.

.... # ....

. . . . # . . . .

Open letter to our waiter, tonight: Weed does not
enhance job performance. Moses spoke to the
burning bush; he didn't smoke it.

. . . . # . . . .

It's easier not to love. Beware of the easy path this day.

. . . . # . . . .

God is moving. When we don't perceive it, it's often an invitation
to slow down.

. . . . # . . . .

.... # ....

If your sin feels "too big," your vision of God is too small.
Reconcile.

.... # ....

Time is the most valuable commodity we have, worth more than
gold, yet wasted more than all else. Efficient use of time begins
with prayer.

.... # ....

Speaking truth will rarely earn you friends, but it will reveal who
your true friends are and who are true friends of Christ.

.... # ....

God, I need a blood transfusion...Your blood, Your grace. Luckily,
Mass starts in 10 minutes (1 Cor 11:23-29).

.... # ....

.... # ....

Asking. Seeking. Knocking. All require effort on our part. #pray

.... # ....

Sunrise & coffee beans, giraffes & platypuses, thunder & lightning, avocados & chili peppers... and, of course, woman...God has style.

.... # ....

Woman is the crown of God's creation, more physiologically complex than a man—blessed to participate, in a special way, in the act of creation with the man and with God. And, speaking as a man, I'm more thankful than I can express that God is so creative.

.... # ....

.... # ....

If I run for office, my platform will include federal funding for every young man to have his very own belt & a penalty if he doesn't use it.

.... # ....

Pondering how Communion is less about our desire to be with God than it is His desire to be with us. #overwhelmed

.... # ....

Gospel truth: if it doesn't require some sacrifice and some suffering...it ain't love.

.... # ....

If you surround your heart with walls, the Lord will send people to knock them down (see Jo 6:20; Heb 11:30).
Lean into His grace...

.... # ....

.... # ....

Honestly, I don't think Victoria has too many Secrets left...might be time to prayerfully consider a name change.

.... # ....

The following is a phrase we don't hear enough but that I sincerely mean (and our culture needs to hear more often): I love being married.

.... # ....

That grass on the other side of the fence? It needs to get mowed, too. Lord, help me to focus on my own lawn today.

.... # ....

Lord, I want to pray for the guy who flipped me off in traffic for letting a car merge into our lane. Bless him, Lord, really, really hard.

.... # ....

.... # ....

Today offers the opportunity for greatness. Sanctity rejects mediocrity.

.... # ....

It's not easy being a father; many days we fail far more than we succeed. Pray for fathers & never underestimate the power of God's grace.

.... # ....

Great lunch. Blessed are the pizza makers, for they shall be called children of God... (Mt 5:9).

.... # ....

Tonight I fixed the staircase, the toilet & the roof. It sounds manly until I mention all these repairs occurred in the Barbie dream house.

.... # ....

118

. . . . # . . . .

Lord, keep me humble. And if I ever actually become humble,
God, keep me from knowing it.

. . . . # . . . .

Hard night tonight. When it's hardest to pray are usually the times
I need to pray the hardest—not sure if that's irony or common
sense.

. . . . # . . . .

There are only 2 things I've learned about following the Holy
Spirit: It will never be easy. It will never be boring.

. . . . # . . . .

It's been a few days since I've seen my kids. My heart's racing; I
can't wait to hold them. This is just a glimpse into God's heart at
Mass

. . . . # . . . .

.... # ....

A homeless man standing at the off-ramp: the question in these moments isn't whether Jesus is in Him, but in me (Mt 25:44-45).

.... # ....

Oh, Coffee, how do I love thee? Let me count the ways...one... hmm...well, one is good enough.

.... # ....

When a majority of my prayers are for others to change, I've gotten off track. Lord, change this sinner's heart.

.... # ....

. . . . # . . . .

If today were your final day of this life, would those things causing you stress still do so? Don't just stop and smell roses...buy them.

. . . . # . . . .

Trying to build the kingdom without the Holy Spirit is like trying to build a skyscraper with Popsicle sticks. #Pentecost

. . . . # . . . .

Many Christians are comfortable with God the Father and Jesus the Son but fear the power of the Holy Spirit. Invite the Holy Spirit into your life and into your day, daily. He is God. He is the most important person in your life. He is pure love.

. . . . # . . . .

.... # ....

If we could see, even for a split second, the depths of God's love for us—all we'd want to do is worship & prayer would never seem a chore.

.... # ....

I need to remember that everyone in that Church, today, has Christ within them—late-comers, early-leavers, non-singers...even the ushers.

.... # ....

At my 3-yr-old's year-end concert. Very off-key, mostly unfocused children but this father is still beaming. Must be how God feels on Sunday.

.... # ....

.... # ....

Gray and overcast...from my earthly perspective, but it's sunny above these storm clouds. Grace lets us see life from God's point of view.

.... # ....

Kids & Suburbs = Biblical: Grocery shopping (Jn 4:8), doing dishes (2 Kgs 21:13b), wiping faces (Bar 6:12), family in a caravan (Lk 2:44).

.... # ....

Phrases I never thought I'd say #162: "Sweetheart, please don't staple your baby sister's hands together...it makes Jesus cry."

.... # ....

I have determined that if we were to remove the word "like" from the English language, my middle-schoolers would be unable to communicate.

.... # ....

. . . . # . . . .

I'm beginning to think that "I haven't had my morning coffee yet" is a Christian way of saying "Back off, pal, you're comin' close to 70 x 7"

. . . . # . . . .

Happy Marriage Tip #257: The correct question isn't "How much did that cost, honey" but, rather, "How did we live so long without it?"

. . . . # . . . .

Rules for today: 1) Pray. 2) Breathe. 3) Repeat. If I stop breathing, I'll see Jesus. If I stop praying...who knows who I'll see.

. . . . # . . . .

How does one discern love? True love works for salvation. If the person, situation or choice does not lead us to salvation...it ain't love.

. . . . # . . . .

.... # ....

Overcommitment can easily become a tool of the devil. Purgatory is filled with souls who did more than God actually asked. We must discern.

.... # ....

Sometimes, out of our great love for God, we actually do "too much." In the process, if God doesn't bless our initiative, we might actually begin to doubt His fidelity. Ask yourself, do I seek God's will before I act or just His approval after I do?

.... # ....

Having a rough day? That's a good sign (Acts 14:22).

.... # ....

.... # ....

Our lives are a living witness to whose glory we seek...ours or His.

.... # ....

Tonight during family prayer, we asked our 3-yr-old where wine comes from. She replied, "Water." Speechless...I've never been more proud.

.... # ....

Lord, thank You for my daughters, their guardian angels...and how the angels don't charge for their services. They worked overtime today.

.... # ....

Spanish teaches us: "el problema" and "la solucion"...the problem is masculine; the solution is feminine. Hmm.

.... # ....

.... # ....

Aquinas: "Perfection of moral virtue does not wholly take away the passions, but regulates them." He then hit the buffet for seconds.

.... # ....

"Daddy, why is Mommy allergic to cats?" "Because God loves me, sweetheart, because God loves me..."

.... # ....

On this Feast of the Annunciation, Lord, give me the grace to need the only being you chose to need so profoundly. Mother Mary, swaddle us.

.... # ....

Don't be the squeaky (whiny) wheel...be God's grease.

.... # ....

127

. . . . # . . . .

"To err is human, to forgive is divine." When we forgive, we act as God acts.

. . . . # . . . .

The command to "love your enemies" (Lk 6:27) sure would be easier if we weren't just starting football season. ;)

. . . . # . . . .

A Sabbath without rest is no Sabbath at all (Mk 2:27-28).

. . . . # . . . .

Time flies. Eternity waits.

. . . . # . . . .

.... # ....

Note to self: You're not an idiot when you make a mistake, you're an idiot when you don't learn from it.

.... # ....

Stop squirming...He's trying to hold you.

.... # ....

Wouldn't our relationship with God be different if we actually took Christ at His Word when He called Him "Abba"?

.... # ....

The Lord has plans to make you a saint today. Let Him.

.... # ....

. . . . # . . . .

If you want to be truly happy, seek first to be truly holy
(Jer 15:16; Mt 6:33).

. . . . # . . . .

If God didn't want us to laugh, He wouldn't have given us a sense
of humor. God laughs (Ps 2:4).

. . . . # . . . .

I've met a lot of people in my life who love God too little, but I've
never met a soul who loved God too much.

. . . . # . . . .

Sssshhh. God is speaking. #Listen

. . . . # . . . .